Don't Scratch
The Diamond

Don't Scratch The Diamond

Reflections on Life, Love and Humanity

DAVID CATRAMBONE

Don't Scratch The Diamond

First Edition
Copyright ©2014 by David Catrambone.
Published by Peace Revolution
Los Angeles, California

All rights reserved. Without limiting the rights under copyright reserved above, no part of this publication may be reproduced, stored in or introduced into a retrieval system, or transmitted, in any form, or by any means (electronic, mechanical, photocopying, recording, or otherwise) without prior written permission of the copyright owner.

ISBN 978-0-692-35781-1

Front and back cover photos by Brian Enright

Dedicated to my dad for passing on the passion of writing and his gift of brevity; and to my mom for giving me life and sharing the beautiful spirit in her heart…

TABLE OF CONTENTS

In this journal-like format, the writings are laid out with a purposeful sense of rhythm, cadence, and wave of emotion. And although there is a general order, I believe the writings are more of a marching procession disclosing more like spiritual life; always at the beginning and willing to walk a path in discovery.

In my own instincts, I find it wildly uncanny how many times I have opened a book to exactly the page and passage I needed to read and feel; my wish is to call to you in a similar fashion. The table of contents speaks under the radar of your own intuition.

Preface	ix
Chapter 1: Illuminations: *Light of Awareness*	1
Chapter 2: Humanity: *Sum of One*	17
Chapter 3: Prose & Poetry: *Dance of Freedom*	29
Chapter 4: Love & Relationships: *Mirror of Being*	51
Chapter 5: Observations: *Mona Lisa's House*	65
Chapter 6: Quotes: *More with Less*	85
About the Author	98

PREFACE

I have always been inspired by writings that unveil awareness to life and offer food for thought in the journey of self-discovery. That journey, to me, has always been elevated by the disciplined art of writing and its tangible experience to learn from. From this engaging vantage point, *Don't Scratch the Diamond* has evolved into a collection of original short writings, poems, and quotes that bring to light and embrace the breadth of humanity in all of its masks and moods. I composed my own sort of poetic philosophy to navigate a way of adapting to life's challenges and changes and to hopefully shed a sliver of light to those whose own library of introspection and wisdom wish to be refreshed and reaffirmed.

I believe that humanity is the diamond: precious, resilient, very hard yet so soft and perpetually dimensional in its sparkle and alluring spell. I have always observed humanity from many different angles and what it relentlessly reflects from each angle is a beauty and a character no less than the previous angle. It is nature's work of art in constant creation with its unique cut and its internal intensity of color aglow through each of us. Like a diamond hardened by the elements of earth and procured within its deep protective layers of time and pressure, humanity too churns in the heart of this great planet and grows in the hearts of all people. No matter how much we misuse our values, our beauty, our traditions, our understandings and misunderstandings, the shine never fades. Life is always testing us to believing in and protecting that unwavering luminosity. You can test the diamond, you can cut the diamond, and you can polish the diamond. Just don't scratch the diamond.

Throughout this incredible writing journey for me, the mysterious flow of life has revealed that we all stand upon our own precipice, peering into the vast world of the unknown tempered with the known sanctuaries of living. With both viewpoints in mind and heart to draw upon, I now invite you to experience the landscape of the written word along with the meditative voice of inspiration to rekindle your own journey of being alive.

David Catrambone

CHAPTER 1 Illuminations

Illuminations
light of awareness

I've been to the breathtaking Hawaiian Islands. Traversed the great trails of the Rocky Mountains. Cruised the stylistic sights of the South of France. Felt the freedom of the vast and sparkling South Pacific. Yet one of the most incredible places to be in the entire world is in the care of someone's thoughts. By far, the most rewarding and longest-lasting endorphin rush comes about by being knowingly thought of.

I was luckily awakened today by the gratitude that this could be my last day. And instead of going into the mind chatter of what my day consists of, I asked first to transform myself into something more aware and more grateful than yesterday. The presence of today's good fortune and revelation should never be taken for granted. For in each waking moment, the promise of another tomorrow must live through the gratitude of another today.

You don't need eyes to see; you need vision and belief. You don't need ears to hear; you need vibration and interpretation. In the moment of each breath, we imagine the world to be beyond our senses and exhale in knowing it is all in the light of imagination.

The stairway to heaven is right here on this amazing earth. There is no rush to pray for some celestial place in the sky to ascend to. No one has come back to tell us that that's the next step. Although we fight each other for heaven's place of meeting and purpose, we are really guessing at this eternal home. All along, beneath our feet, where the dust of humanity layers the earth, our footsteps imbed the evidence and reminiscence of being here; perhaps even foster the rich soil of never leaving. Earth has given us everything we could ever need and desire and asks nothing in return. So before the next step on this stairway, revisit what constant life force has been and will always be your home along this fragile and beautiful mystery to heaven.

Today did not go as planned. In fact, everything seemed to just miss its mark. Some days you only have control over the loss of control. Once you give in, the certainty of uncertainty unfolds just as planned.

Words are a tricky matter; sometimes they mean what you say and then sometimes are just mean in what they say. Sometimes more words count less. Sometimes less words count more. Words are always a fine balance of the compliment of difficult and easy. Like most things in life, it's not quantity; it's quality in the trickiest of ways.

I believe in having money for its usefulness. Yet your net-worth is not the same thing as your self-worth and your value is not based on your valuables. So use the service of money for the things you need but not above the value and respect of yourself and the life of others.

Fear instructs us on what to let go of and not what to hang on to.

Fear stirs the core of your being and acts as a conduit for a new outlook and approach.

Fear is not resistance; it is relinquishing in its disguise.

Fear is not about being limited; it is awakening us to our limitlessness.

Fear never sleeps; it is too afraid of missing a moment of possible stimulation.

Fear never dreams; for dreams are the fire and passion that pulse through its veins.

And fear never ever doubts itself; it leaves that fear up to us.

The only thing that comes after you pick a fruit while it is still green is the outcome of waste. Haste never advances the process; it just sets you back at the beginning of temptation.

∽ Illuminations: *light of awareness*

Living in a culture marinated in speed and processed in abundance, life can be congested and complicated. The feeling of being constantly overwhelmed takes its toll and disconnects us to love, family, and all relationships in general. Some days you just want to stop the spinning and slow down enough to realize you are breathing and what that sounds like and feels like. In every life there is a need to return to the simplicity of stillness; the antidote to what we cook ourselves in. It is amazing what gets done when you allow yourself to be undone.

Just dreaming of the white snow's reviving reflection and magnetism among other things from afar. I love those nights when the crisp cold air fills your being and ignites you vibrantly alive from head to toe. The mountains always offer such a balance of power and peaceful wonder. May you unveil your own wonder in a night sky that rains with stars and whispers sweet dreams.

✧✧✧

In my mind of plenty and seemingly plenty more, where the many in thought eventually whittle down to the very rare few in heart: in one good woman you experience the entire female race.

In all relationships you have to distinguish between the transient and the enduring. There is always the realization that you have been through this all before and now face the moment to having what it takes to go beyond it.

Seems we are inclined to take away from those that have too little and give more to those who already have too much. Even though the scales of balance appear lopsided, the belief that you have everything when you can be happy to have nothing is all the leverage you need.

∼ ILLUMINATIONS: *light of awareness*

It is always enlightening to take inventory of your life to see what you have and don't have; to find what is working, what is unnecessary, and exactly what internal dialogue you are listening to and following through in action. The realization of being grateful for what you have and grateful for what you don't have is reflected by the process of looking within. In the end though, to give of you is all you really reflect and ultimately leave behind for others to take inventory of.

The morning sun has unveiled that what you seek is already within you and awaits release. Seems everything happens for you--and not to you-- at exactly the right moment just as the sky opens with its fanning rays of light to embrace all uncertainties.

There is so much beauty in the world; before me, behind me, and around me in every direction. Each day a rising wonder makes certain to light the way with an energy and warmth in unrivaled plentitude. And as the day relinquishes to night, I surrender into slumber never doubting the beauty that will greet me once again to another awakening.

In reaching a thought's end, sometimes the farther you go, the less you know. And the end reveals but again the beginning of thought.

In spiritual thought you are always at the beginning of freedom. There is nowhere to go nor any place to end. An eternal home-- no questions asked and no reaching thoughts to resolve.

~ ILLUMINATIONS: *light of awareness*

In the dark face of adversity we have the opportunity to alight a new expression of gratefulness. There is always a lesson in what we do not know. The shadow of fear seems to dissipate with the radiance of each new day bowing before the expanse of the universe.

I make mistakes. You make mistakes. They make mistakes. We all make mistakes. In fact, you probably are not alive without experiencing a lot of mistakes. But mistakes are forgivable and forgettable and not something you hold on to. And if I'm not mistaken, you actually can offer up your mistakes as collateral for the door that opens the next window of opportunity.

It's hard to fathom that in the panic of uncertainty and scarcity, you can utilize not only a still speculative mind but also the incredible power of fearlessness to move beyond any obstacle. You don't have to break through an obstacle; the obstacle breaks through your own trust of undoing its interference.

What if you were free to say exactly what you mean unburdened by fears or awkward complications? Freedom of expression is the Creator's fluid language and gift to us; like opening the window and listening to the wind while talking to the stars.

You can be a host to the Creator or a hostage to ego. The latter enslaves a very small self- centered planet while the former rejoices in a self-correcting blissful universe.

Law governs the path to the material plane.
What you see is what you can collect.

The path to the spiritual plane, lawlessness.
What you don't see is your choice to believe.
Faith is not blind, it's visionary.

Perhaps heaven's placement of the stars is aligning in some favorable vortex and divinity and will sprinkle magic on all our lives. I hope so. Life is always reaffirming when miracles unfold; it sheds a lustrous light on this great mystery we are all traveling through.

The drought is over. The sky fills its space with the abundance of unprecedented downpour. I open myself to fill the well in which nourishment and activation celebrate in tandem movement. I feel a change as a light sprinkle builds to a constant fall from heaven's tears. The rain pelts my being in defiance of not being denied, heard, and felt. Like a sponge, my soul accepts this watering after years on end of impenetrability and insatiability. The doors of love, of spirit, of a heart wanting to be used, and the willingness of will open for inclusion. Its forecast is to let nothing scare you. Let nothing trouble you. To let yourself be taken in its flowing prayer. So stand naked to the sky and feel the rain wash away all skepticism and inject a relentless drenching of love.

∼ ILLUMINATIONS: *light of awareness*

The power of an unwavering belief can often inspire and trigger a tangible outcome. Life is a reflection of what you believe and wish to be aligned with. To the shedding of an old skin and the emergence of a new pair of eyes and open heart that ignite a radiant new beginning.

Life isn't all about you. It's more about what circulates in and around your being. It's about the beat your heart acknowledges. It's about the stillness that connects you to everything and everyone alive. It's about the good fortune that flows despite the troubled waters of your own doing. It's the bridge you make with those that have traveled the same path and now stand at this mirrored awareness to leaving all egoic ways behind.

CHAPTER 2 Humanity

Humanity
sum of one

We have to be continually aware of raising our fellow brothers and sisters with the passing on of intimacy, love, and compassion. Collectively we cannot let this fade or be pushed aside by indolence. Each of us is capable of nurturing these virtues. Never lose hope of being better than what you are in each opportunistic and challenging moment. We are all a part of the same sacrifice to keep togetherness alive.

Heroes come in many styles, sounds, and colors. Some quiet and unassuming, some thrust into improbable situations, some outcomes big as life, and some even bigger than life. However, more times than not, it's the everyday individual dealing with the challenge of the present moment that seems to collectively register the biggest roar of a hero's conquest.

A day of frolicking in the radiance of nature ushered in soft winds lustfully playing in the trees and endless images emerging from clouds in the blue dream of sky. Nature seems always to heal and give strength to body and soul; a real infusion of medicine not found in any drug store. The human spirit needs places where nature has not been rearranged by the hands of people. What's left untouched allows a wake of beauty to announce the setting sun's whisper and vow for another tomorrow.

With an insane amount of chatter and unrest, this past year seemed like the longest journey going from the head to the heart. Hopefully this new chapter will start in the heart of compassion and ignite the extension of civility in all of us. We could all hold each other a little dearer and be a touch more understanding, patient and kind. So sip the tears of someone you love and relish in the comfort and closeness of being gratefully human.

We all suffer; rich, poor, male, female, fortunate and unfortunate. It is a prerequisite for living and no one is spared. Yet despite the wide variety of circumstances, we still all have the same challenge: to use suffering to find a place of peace from which not to suffer from.

We appear to be at our most creative when figuring out ways of destroying each other. It's a bit mind-blowing that the collection of great minds and energy unfortunately focus on dark, downtrodden outcomes. Don't get me wrong, I believe in creativity; I also believe in protecting and defending ourselves. What I don't believe is that we can't find another way to channel the feeling alive without destroying the path to getting there.

We are moving much too fast to notice ourselves in the act of life. So stop a moment…and be not afraid of the quiet voice that is masked in overwhelming chatter… then step into the day with a conscious offering; one of kindness, caring, or even the extension to help another breathe a little easier for a moment. The conduit to goodwill lives and breathes in all of us.

I have learned silence from the talkative; compassion from the complainer; kindness from the mean-spirited; gentleness from the aggressor; fairness from the disrespectful. I find it humbling and most interesting how we learn from those we least expect to teach us.

No matter what corner of the earth we travel to there is an inherent constant among people: in the display of emotions, all tears and joys flow clearly transparent… and in the mirror of our differences, we still all bleed the same color.

We don't need more laws; we need more accountable leaders.

We don't need more debates; we need more intelligent decisions.

We don't need more machines; we need more ingenuity to activate people.

We don't need more possessions; we need more giving of our abundances.

We don't need more news; we need more transparent truths.

We don't need more technology; we need more human touch and contact.

We don't need more wealth; we need more priceless compassion.

We don't need more borders; we need more boundless freedoms.

We don't need more judgments; we need more open acceptance.

We don't need more than what we need,
We just need more than what we don't have.

✧✧✧

The universal struggle to attaining peace as people is unending. We all should make an extra effort to contribute to this calming agent and ally. After all, bliss is a habit we can cultivate and surely wish abundantly upon one another.

Each of us is an original painting; in style, in tone, in color. We show everything we are and are not in each brushstroke. So observe, honor, and let it be. For no one can repaint the true colors of another human being.

It is in our differences that we find sameness, in our misunderstandings we find understanding, and in our darkest seeded ignorance that we find a spirit that embraces the open heart of compassion.

The act and art of connecting to others is in a suspended animation and a form of hiatus today in our world. Somehow we forgot to affirm that "friction" between people is a springboard for communication and a meeting ground for mutual understanding. I am still perplexed how the act of flirting with a live person has been substituted with the sterile, technological skin of a cell phone. I am all for change and advancement and know the roles of men and women are all being reworked, but really, a cell phone? So for a day, try connecting differently and get off the grid and put that cell phone away. Be bold and courageous and step into the world unarmed and unattached to any technological gadget. And look someone in the eyes; dial them in. They could be not only a great person but also the best life--and screen-- saver you could ever call on.

Character is how you treat those who can do nothing for you. It reflects humanity through accepting all circumstances with acts of blind compassion; like looking in the mirror and feeling yourself in the faces of many other people.

We all meander in judging others and comparing our life to theirs, which usually leads to a form of turbulence. How gracefully you let go of things not meant for you allow judging and comparing to transform into well wishes for others and paves a peaceful wandering in your every step.

∽ Humanity: *sum of one*

Some offerings and wishes to fulfill…

Don't be afraid
We are all right here
To hold an open hand
To kiss someone with kindness
To grab the moment with life's force, both
strong and gentle
To not squander your power, nor squash your dreams,
but to share and celebrate both as if your
last dance was called
To ask divine intervention in reminding us daily that
thoughtfulness is the river of humanity and the essence
that flows through all our veins
Remember to not accept what is unacceptable and trust
your convictions
To believe in extraordinary love as anything less will
not fuel your soul to soar
Pray for women to rediscover their femininity
Pray for men to rediscover their virility
And pray that children witness the difference
and adopt the beautiful balance and compliment both
aspects offer
Pray to help wherever you can, to heal whomever you
can, and to forgive everything and everyone that camp
in your being
To health, peace of mind, and the spirit that connects
us unconditionally to this magnificent world.

CHAPTER 3 Prose & Poetry

Prose & Poetry
dance of freedom

You read my writings, my thoughts, and imagine how I feel by the stitching of my words. You feel our similarities, our differences, and our triumphant struggles. You find me hiding in my darkest night and sleepless in the brightest of new beginnings. Near or far, what I feel, somehow you feel. We are not all that different. So when you read my writings, the door is always open to sharing. Sometimes the most beautiful language communicated is in-between the lines unspoken.

In knowing that one has applied the heart's magnificence without fear, the heart beats on as a tenacious hunter. The vulnerabilities transform into surges of passion, the heartaches turn to wisdom, and the disappointments tranquil the blood so no restrictions diminish the heart's openness. The heart needs no protection; it desires to be utilized not immobilized. And even though one feels the pang of exposing the heart, it's only a brief moment until the next wave of excitation fills the emptiness of vulnerability with the fullness of unstoppable fury.

Don't Scratch The Diamond

And if all the world were a rhyme…

We'd see and feel a constant harmony
weave its web of time.

With ebb and flow a forever delight
and mother and child an incandescent light.

With no heaven or hell to compare our ends,
no fighting or killing of earth's living friends.

Life seems all for nothing and then nothing for all,
with trials and sacrifices that paint each mythical call.

An unwavering belief to bring forth our true spirit,
a triumph that sings in the key to pursue it.

To the wonders unknown and always mysterious,
we ask our questions but remain oh so curious.

To a falling star that confirms all you intuit,
and that kind gentle voice that assures always
you knew it.

To realize our limited fragile powers,
to endure with courage in faith's waning hours.

Is it all worth the grief, struggle and pain?
– why of course, says the "I" that straddles insane.

If I had one chance, one wish to instill,
I'd fathom the moment and pour forth all my will.

For in the brief moment when day surrenders to night,
a captive in my heart will keep always alight.

For in life's essence there will be a few secrets to
trigger wonder, I surrender to my soul and the
silence after thunder.

For if all the world were a rhyme, we'd share in peace
and live forever lasting this moment in time.

Don't Scratch The Diamond

There are moments when I am not sure where the next breath will come from; moments where time and motion stands still yet remains so fluidly perpetual in togetherness; moments where preoccupation and pain can only be soothed and restored by the source from which it came; moments where dreams and wishes color the sky with an original stroke and flow of heaven's brush; moments that reveal a vast ocean of love and peace and blissful aliveness; and moments that I pause in captive silent stillness, to marvel in the precious chance to breathe.

I rest myself down on the mountain with the brilliant sun bringing warmth to ancient bones. The nearing end of winter is a welcomed feeling and notion of passing. With the greatest of ease, my friends of nature reflect once again, the mirror that I am, and follow in process. With each season I find my own cycles of living more directed on the path of nature's way. I can withdraw, I can emerge, I can die, or I can celebrate-- all in tune with the open arms and all knowing ways of nature. This is my home. There are no other destinations, only this journey in step with change and my divine heritage.

She is as beautiful as the day that greets the universe; as soft as clouds that kiss us with rain; as sensual as silk sliding down a bare-naked thigh; as captivating as the silence in the aftermath of sighs. I can hear her sweet voice; I can feel her hunger lust over my body. I witness her sexy prowl as she brushes her scent against me claiming me captive; her searing heat as she undulates before me. She fits into my displacement of shape; she is the yin to my yang, the dark to my light, the complete to my incomplete, the twist to my turn and the song to my beat. Like a star streaking across the sky, her radiance overwhelms my being and I surrender to tell her as my eyes lock on hers; that today I find a love before me and if tomorrow never came anew, I would always hold the moment that a beautiful love passed me into the open arms of you.

There is a natural tendency for day to relinquish its light to night; a vow of camaraderie and trust to benefit each other's rightful passage. The sun setting and the witching hour rising is a sign that all things must endure. For in the light, there awaits darkness, and in the darkness, there awaits light. Everything seems complete when the sky's brilliant face turns dim and the earth's surface welcomes another night to nurture its blackness.

All that is struggling to attain form is beset with difficulties. Growth takes on many faces and moods. In each, a constant change to further life and existence. Nurtured in the dimness of the underground, the blade of grass punctures its way through the earth's soil to challenge light; a heroic moment that comes to visible life. The initiation can only be seen as a naturally beautiful emergence. The grace to live and the grace to die await its order. As with everything, there is a time, there is a place, and there is an expression and aggression we grieve to achieve.

Why do I feel so alive amidst the chaos of it all?
Is there really any sense of order or must I find my way home in each breath?
Why do I understand so much about so little?
Could there be any more to know other than the selfless act to accept?
Why do I question what my heart tells my eyes?
Is there really any other answer beside the truest beat of life?
Why do I listen to the cluttering chatter of others?
Could it sway open the door to a silence of incessant fortitude?
Why do I care about the reflection of another?
Is there a mirror that reflects back a greater radiance?
Why do I love and want to be loved? Could the fear of emptiness propel me close to a more personal, yet shared bliss?
Why do I feel so alive amidst the chaos of it all?
Perhaps life simply whispers a window of awareness and acceptance upon those whom listen to the gentle voice of turmoil.

Like the light that fills the void in wandering night, where its pleasure is to pour forth its unyielding splendor upon the beat that rules my heart, I call for the stars to announce your breath upon my yearning ears in the silence of the moment. I call to the hidden moon to unveil your eyes and alight the deepest daring part of me when rendered by the voltage of your gaze. I call to the winds for bringing your skin's softness and the invite to touch not only your radiance but to taste what savors on savors' lips. For what could be more delectable than to have your essence as an everlasting aftertaste? And as my hands now grasp all of your being, I am certain to exist. As in all my wildest calls for you, I can only cradle your magnificence just as the day envelops the universe--in grand openness, in utter wonder, in favor of only favor, and in tune with the love that fills the void of darkness with a brilliant aura of my beating heart against yours.

∽ PROSE & POETRY: *dance of freedom*

The conservation of winter's energy always relinquishes itself to a new form in the unfolding of spring. A season of rebirth, of seed progression to flower, of the ritual passage in shedding a skin of the past and being naked to the virgin rays of the sun's vital nourishment is always welcomed. We all perpetually rise from our own ashes in the surrendering to being and becoming. To begin again is a natural gift and a powerful sign that we are alive and once again receptive. I embrace this season and the radiance of every living thing in this moveable feast; the kaleidoscope of blooms, the meandering lure of scents, the love songs and exchanges of the free and wild, and all the beautiful women framed in grace and irresistible enticement. In wearing my own colorful cloak of renewal and gratitude, I now offer to you: a spring dance of blessings and secret whispers that unveil your heart and feverishly arouse the sleeping fire from within.

The contrasting duality of everything continues to present its case to all observations: I am happy, I am sad; I am fulfilled, I am lonely; I am restless, I am surrendered to sleep; I am fertile, I am empty; I am expanded by the experiences, I am contracted by the so very little that happens; I am loved, I am unseen; I am willing, I am uncommitted; I am dreaming, I am too conscious; I am light, I am dark; I am unending, I am always at the beginning; I am, am I? When all is said and done, to simply realize that the first ray of daylight born from the last breathless bolt of night is the most deserving observation of them all.

There is a time to be together and a time to be apart,
There is an instant when I touch you and it sparks again my heart.
There is no word for you I can summon, only a current to weave its way,
There is a feeling I've reencountered and it speaks of you today.

There is your gaze I often feel, your voice a
melodious song,
There is a life force you so radiate and the
laughter to belong.
There is your heart, a path so willing, in its surge
to nourish my skin,
There is a grace and bond in the offering and a
love to endure endlessly in.

Be it the moon on this full night,
be it the last breath for life to live,
Be it the lone shining star in the towering stretch
of sky, or be it this blessing to give.
For there is a gift I sprinkle to be shared, a seed for a
bloom unknown,
There is a season that encircles to hold you, and a
dancing spirit to be sown.
There is a time to be together and a time to be apart,
in each, a peace for all it's worth,
And there is now a kiss I deliver to you with our
love to reign on earth.

The most radiant part of your being is love. Unexplainable and certainly indefinable, we all attempt to give love a purpose, and in the highest sense, a respect to set in order the complexities of our lives. For love is there to balance and to make clear what we truly have to offer to one another. There is no other face so awesomely arrayed as love. Love does conquer all. Love unites us as equals, never behind or ahead of anything. Love, after the smoke and illusion fade, presents a presence unaltered. Love's patient and persistent workings break down any wrong doings and misgiving. Love somehow never seems to be hurt or slighted or leaning to one side. Love is favor. Love is choice. Love is conviction. Love lasts even after you thought it was gone. Love fills the oceans and shapes the mountains and is constant as the elemental cycles and undoubtedly the wind's kiss that keeps them circulating. Love understands the misunderstandings and never gives up on itself. Love is being open and not closing the door to difficult circumstances. Love is never afraid to love. Love is the breath you feel deep in your being on a clear crisp day. Love is the common bond you recognize when you peer into another's eyes. Love is Mom. Love is Dad. Love is Sister and Brother and friend and lover. Love lets you sleep in the comfort of your family. Love is family. Love is tribal. Love is simply love; it has no end and begins always where it has just touched and given of itself.

That night we kissed; I left a poem in your mouth. The first few lines told of the softest lips bestowed to man; and in that contact, the exchange of a language connecting us to something even greater than imagined. This meeting of lips, of submissive tongues, of the primal pleasures in shared breath, was a testament to the rhyme and resonance of life, the poem echoed. Then your lips locked me in succulent arrest; and the real dance began. Even with eyes shut, I could see forever in you; the merging of our skin like the titanic pull of celestial forces in the sky. I found to be willingly lost in your hum that resonated inside my mouth and flowed with the swishing transfer of energies and desires so remarkable, like the light years between here and infinity. And in a heightened pause from the moment, I opened my eyes and found a peaceful, quiet sensation as I fell into you and you landed tenderly upon me. Now, even from afar on each unfolding night, I can hear the lines of the poem sing and dance every time you exhale as the breath of you kisses the breath of me.

How is it that...
… in one tear the emotion of an entire lifetime is released?
… in one small standing pool of water the seamless sky reflects its vastness?
… in one kiss that all stress and uncertainty exits your body?
… in one compliment everything is renewed, attainable, and forgivable?
… in one moment an entire future is foretold?
By recognizing the nuances in living you actually breathe life into it.
A beautiful thing happens when we pay attention to each other and the moments of life that bring us together in one.

In every fiber of my being there resonates a gentle hymn of you inside as if a seed of creation has placed itself in the center of my life force and ignited the activation pulse. In this voltage is an incredibly powerful surge that brings all things together and within touch by the tune of you. Like the celestial clock that follows the forces of what always has been, I find you in everything. With each step toward our next encounter, a graceful vibration of you illuminates and echoes in a silent sea of everywhere.

My bed is alone and empty
Yet my heart is contentedly teeming
My hands move to hold but feel nothing
Yet grasp every inch of your being

My body writhes in hopeful fervor
Yet feels only truly alive when pressed safe against yours
My whispers sing and dance with desire
Yet in your absence incomplete as it roars

My mind races in wanting destination
Yet in stillness reveals what is real
My thoughts flower in your radiant presence
Yet linger longer with repeating appeal

The day is near over
The night befriends the dawn
The ticking time is no longer
And with you is where I belong
My bed is alone and empty
Yet my heart is contentedly teeming
For I now rest to dream of the moment
When our lips greet again for love's meeting.

I will pass on too, one day. No longer in the flesh to feel the chill of being alive or feeling the rapture that runs rampant through my heart. How incredibly precious to fathom the beat of life. Will I generate the emotion to cry once I've left or to feel so heavenly guttural in my laughter? Will I want to give all I can or is all this a formula to formulate letting it all go? And when my presence no longer holds the human form, who will see me? And will there be someone there to greet me "hello- how are you today"? Or does my human ghost continue into solitude, completely unattached to all I ever knew? Will anyone miss me or the sight of me once I step into the unknown? How is it that we are all replaceable? Does anyone who has left mind being replaced? With that, and this moment of stillness, I take a deep breath because I am still here and there's truly nothing to miss only to question. But I do wonder if I'll miss myself? Or will I be irretrievably lost and free enough to turn my ghosts into angels and my angels into dreams unimagined?

How much longer must I wait to see you?
The walls of winter, now bleeding with longing due
Shedding the skin of darkness
So that light can reveal me to you
How much longer must I wait to touch you?
As spring feels only right, bathing you in its glow
Waking the sun of rebirth
And the kiss of life to you I sow
In your eyes, a galaxy
Where all stars perfectly align
And the rushing breath of your heart
Rides on the wind that I now claim as mine
For all the days have turned to nights
And all the nights have turned to you
In every season that yields to another
There is a turn that turns for loving you

How much longer must I wait to hold you?
The summer's heat, now dripping in yearning blues
Melting the distance between us as my hands merge into my beautiful muse
How much longer must I wait to see you?
As fall's release, dropping what's no longer anew
Fluttering are the leaves so freely
And the knowing they will land upon you

Don't Scratch The Diamond

In your eyes, a galaxy
Where all stars perfectly align
And the rushing breath of your heart
Rides on the wind that I now claim as mine
For all the days have turned to nights
And all the nights have turned to you
In every season that yields to another
There is a turn that turns for loving you.

I had the great fortune of stepping into the mountains today. Besides touching the softened earth once again, the air that filled the sky was like a newborn's first breath; fresh and charged with the abundance of life. Harmony blanketed everything and kissed alive each rain-washed leaf, branch, rock, and vibrant green blade of grass. The water tributaries rushed down the hills and trickled through rocks in search of inclusion in the river below. To be a part of the magnificent flow was its purpose and undeniable yearning. There were clouds dancing in the turquoise sky, and hawks flying from tree to tree in some playful game as their red tails glistened in the sun. At moments, the wind would forcefully gust and crescendo and the entire forest would sway in rhythm, relinquishing beads of water that fell onto a once-upon-a-time world. Even the trees sang in rejoice and were complimented by the brilliant sunlight that had been hidden for day's prior. The entire scenario was nature at its finest and most captivating in every sense. I sat and pictured you in the breathtaking trees and mountains, in the river's flow, the dancing clouds, the hawk's flight of freedom and finesse, and the green rolling valley where your velvety ivory skin would contrast and compliment this grand work of art. Upon feeling so incredibly complete, I now step again into these magical mountains knowing you are the rain that makes everything gracefully come to life.

People are what I feel deep within along with the reassurance of life from those who have passed on. I find myself so alive in writing this as I gander at the movement of my hand and see a timeless motion of men; I am one. I have helped perpetuate our energy and spirit. My hands have touched the most beautiful of creations, the most incredible of moments throughout history. I've built pyramids and have drawn fish out of the Nile. I've caressed the finest lines of Cleopatra. I've touched a child and healed for the moment, its pain. My mind's eye designed the timeless structures of Rome, composed music that still sings aloud today, and my heart, eagerly beat to the gallop of the night's horsemen. I find a treasure of feelings in this deep well and I share my find with our entire passing.

Life feels odd at moments. To be in tune with lunacy tempers my spirit. Such vast incongruencies and polarities stretch in-between this phase of the moon. Am I coming or going and does it favor any certain unknown? At times I feel a part of it all. And other times, I feel all apart. In all its peculiarities, the form and life of thought need only be expressed, for it can never be fully extinguished.

CHAPTER 4 Love & Relationships

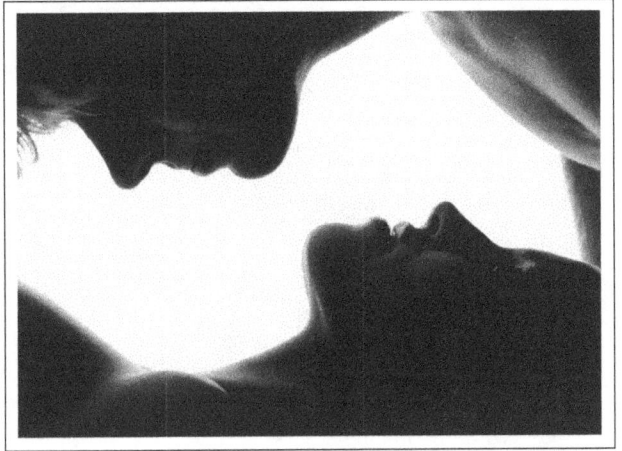

Love & Relationships
mirror of being

∽ LOVE & RELATIONSHIPS: *mirror of being*

The Troubadours of the 12th century had an incredible vision to offer. After centuries of arranged meetings and marriages, they initiated the idea of love as a person-to-person relationship. Their idea of romantic love gave individuals the right and choice to be with whom they wanted. At the time, this exchange was quite radical as it gave power to the individual's selection opposed to giving all the power to the traditional arrangements by families and society. It was the start of owning our own ideal of love and elevated the notion of person-to-person to a higher spiritual value. And even though we have practiced this for some 800 years now, we are still working out the kinks…in every sense of the word. Propelling the idea of love as a sacred and very intimate choice between two people is quite the gift to have been gifted.

Most people design their life around finding a mate; a companion that makes one feel complete and a reflective witness of a life experienced and lived well. We go to the ends of the earth and depths of our souls to make this connection a reality. There seems no greater drive or fulfillment than that of loving and being loved by someone special. Yet woven so masterfully in this fulfillment is not only your quest for finding the love of your life but discovering the life of your love.

I remember the first time I felt you.
I remember whispering into your ear and sensing your eyes translate every nuance of sound.
I remember my hands holding your face and watching the softness of your lips take me far, faraway yet draw me closer into a kiss.
I remember the night I held you in my arms when no one else existed nor walked on the planet. We shared

Love & Relationships: *mirror of being*

everywhere and everything at the same instant.
I remember confessing our truths and appreciation of each other and knowing I was safe and you were secure in whatever expression we uttered.
I remember grabbing your hand and being connected to everything alive.
I remember the first touch of your skin and the last contact of my fingertip's trace.
I remember reading your thoughts as you read my wildest intentions.
I remember awakening to your loving eyes and feeling I was home.
I remember how I loved you with all my heart and lucky enough to tell you as I wiped the tears of joy from your beautiful face…
And now, as those memories fade along with the realization that I cannot piece together what has splintered in countless directions, I don't know what will stay alive in my memory banks. But I do know in every part of me how you made me feel; I will never ever forget to remember that feeling.

Your allure held my every move with a knowing resistance. I wanted to envelop you with how you made me feel. I wanted to tug on your hair and drink from your intoxicating essence. It took all my might to not touch you…Yet once my hands cradle your face, your lips will only be mine and my kiss will be only yours to make the body weak and the heart strong. On the trembling lips of your heated breath, I now taste every resistant desire that only a kiss sets aflame.

My fingers gently tug the gorgeous curls of your flowing radiant hair. With each new handful, a flowering scent emanates off your silky skin and summons my lips to taste yours. As I glide and lick over your wonder, I feel your magical eyes pull me back to your calling breath. I could spend an eternity listening to your breath as it christens my face in exhale. I meet your eyes again and now realize, I am in eternity.

∼ LOVE & RELATIONSHIPS: *mirror of being*

In a healthy order of this universe a man needs to respect a woman; but a woman has to give a man something to respect. The compliment to our connectivity is in knowing and honoring what each state of respect offers. A woman's gift is to shower with care in opening and closing the gates of heaven. A man's gift is to trust with conviction in giving a woman the keys to care for all living things. Maybe we can start there and funnel our natural energies into a respectful order.

Life will break you. A relationship will break you. Solitude will break you. A crowded room of people will break you. And even though your heart will at some point break, you still need and crave someone else's heart to help unbreak your own.

I have you in my thoughts on this seamless deep sapphire night. And I wonder how you are and where you are knowing we share the same sky above and common earth beneath our feet. I surmise at this moment the only thing that separates us is what story we tell ourselves in connecting the stars lighted words. And then, I believe, it is that coded illumination that unites us… Your sunset photo was inspiring; a moment bathed in shades of orange and crimson vicariousness. It is amazing how witnessing that magnificence never depletes the eyes and heart while enveloping one's stillness. It is good to be present and you captured that moment beautifully. So on this night, where I find myself falling into your eyes, my wishes embrace you from afar and say simply yet longingly goodnight.

LOVE & RELATIONSHIPS: *mirror of being*

Your face was the light that chased away the shadows and fears
Your voice displaced sound and made music of my dissonance
You reminded me that love is simple in unifying and in overcoming separation; and that we are in the world to help one another, not to condemn one another.
Your eyes spoke of romance and opened again my ache for co-adventure
Your whispers held me still and trained me to love the light of my own darkness
You reminded me that although uncertainty is a constant companion we are all really just a bridge to someone or somewhere else.
And the moment you realize that no one is your enemy, except yourself, resistance dissipates and another new bridge appears.
I loved the days when we filled in each other's incompleteness and the nights our bodies merged into perfect compliment. In my zealous attempt of trying to make you more a part of me than I am myself, I call to you again insatiably thirsty; for your character, for your wisdom, and for your presence that always showers me in sweet refrain.

✧✧✧

I love the indulgence of exploring someone in a relationship; to let the floodgates open and to be raw in overflowing vulnerabilities and sensations. It's liberating to have the conviction that to wear yourself out is to be new again. It also takes courage to stand at the edge of the precipice and decide to jump freely into the unknown of another. For how often does "chemistry" ignite that internal passion to leap? I believe in being bold and daring in loving someone; for that is what passion requires and because really all you have to lose comes around in another form. Some lovers are content longing. I am content loving. I want to be engulfed in the bliss of having you writhe and whisper "again"… and again…and again.

It's the endings of relationships that we're unprepared for in life. You can see them coming and know they are for the better, yet are still dazed by their reality. After some effort, time, and working through the ball of emotions, the one epiphany I had was that it was fairly easy to actually watch her leave my life under the circumstances. What I was completely unprepared for was how tough it was to get her to leave my thoughts long after she was gone.

∽ LOVE & RELATIONSHIPS: *mirror of being*

I have come full circle to realize that being in a deeply fulfilling relationship with you is not about you giving me what I want; it's about you enhancing the part of me that feels inspired to give back to you my undivided attention and love.

He's in love with her and she's in love with him. But they're not in love with each other. You witness it more than not. The deep well of love to draw from seems almost endless to tap. But it is the deep well of sacrifice that is far more difficult to draw from. Loving someone is easy but if you are not willing to sacrifice for the relationship and commit to what that entails, then loving that person fades. Look at the divorce rate today; there cannot be that many people picking the wrong mate. They just may be picking love before understanding sacrifice.

✧✧✧

You have to find in the core of your being, which dreams to fight for and which dreams to oppose in allowing your spirit to sing. In the sharing of dreams with a partner, it is equally important to know which dreams will enhance happiness and which dreams will deflate happiness. You have to be careful to not destroy each other's dreams. Life is so very delicate and dreams are the backbone of a life well lived and illustriously shared.

The night's chill has crawled through my window and announced a familiar change of season; where darkness now dominates and light relinquishes its sovereignty. In my retreat, sometimes I write to be close to you; sometimes I write to comfort you; sometimes I write because I have you not near to hear my whispers… yet all the time I write to remind myself of just how magical you are, wherever you may be, and wherever your sweet dreams will lead you in hopes that they all lead you to me…on this chilly night when all I can think of and dream of is you.

◡ Love & Relationships: *mirror of being*

Most of us are gluttons for punishment. It's usually from losing control or feeling rejection and we find it conveniently compelling to keep hitting our head against a situation or a person. The outcome usually winds up at the same dead end. So I decided to break my own punishment patterns and weaknesses and ransacked all my electronic memories: emails, texts, photos, videos, and IMs and deleted them all. I felt liberated and freed myself of her and the pain, I thought. And then I got strangely sentimental, then depressed, and threw out all her wine glasses just to hear my heart break all over again.

In his own quiet way, he affirmed me. Never to gain attention, nor boast on how he felt, he honored me. He told his dreams for me in many actions but in few words; they were subtle hints with loud overtones. I did not listen to all he said. I was not fully aware of his dreams for me while trying to figure out my own dreams for myself. He saw something special in me that I didn't see in myself. And as I look back, he knew me better than I knew of myself in what gifts I could offer and share. He never tried to change my individuality; he saw what made me unique. And although he never said how proud of me he was, I still feel his dreams, I still feel his spirit, and I still feel affirmed by the many ways my dad loved me and made me feel whole.

CHAPTER 5 Observations

Observations
mona lisa's house

Life always boils down to the energy you have; to nurture, to share, to sustain life. And although this energy seems to be an endless well to draw from, you only have a finite amount of time to tap it and to fulfill life's dreams and aspirations. So while you have access to this great resource, don't just give it away or misuse it frivolously; harness it and respect its power. For energy is not only the fountain of youth, but also the fountain of living as we know it.

It is the possibility of having a dream come true that makes life interesting and surprising; to wipe clean the sky and paint your most intimate dreams in pastels shades of fruition honors always your belief and even more so, your essence. So tell the eternal sky all your dreams and rejoice in hearing it sung by the sea of unknown yet familiar voices.

A radiant and plentiful sun in tandem with a wild and restless wind twists a warm winter day in southern California. A good moment, a good day, a good season to cast one's own new story and personal myth along with the momentum of elemental alchemy. After all, there are countless ways to kneel and kiss the ground and ask for the universe's guidance and blessings to be born again and again.

Every mood of the heart influences us to movement in pain and in passion; a constant beat keeping track of life. As life is realized in the acts of life, the heart keeps company; ardent and forever striving for fulfillment, for desires tangible, and for the freedom to sing its song softly and endlessly with each and every impulse of life.

∾ OBSERVATIONS: *mona lisa's house*

In the stillness that precedes a tropical storm, I witness the rush of clouds merging for downpour. And though the wind swirls in syncopation, it also breeds a deafening silence. In that quiet vacuum, I am instantly shaken…and reminded that it is the rumble of thunder that aligns me for the nourishment of rain.

Positive vibrations seem always to resonate when courage fills the heart and connects vulnerability to worthiness and worthiness to compassion. It's a cycle that feeds and insulates itself where fear has no place to enter. We take flight when the strength of our passion exceeds the strength of our blockages. Kind of like going back to the state of mind you had as a child when you believed nothing was impossible because nothing was in your way.

Can I have a minute of your time? Actually, no. Eight seconds is today's average attention span. A goldfish has a nine second average attention span. We have trained our minds to hear what is said but have not generated any capacity to listen. If you don't believe me, just ask a goldfish.

We need an antidote to the counterfeit love going around. Perhaps we should start marketing the idea that dedication is sexy, the expression of truth is hot, the mutual respect of communication engaging, and the sharing of positive thoughts and actions, life changing. We should push for a platform of these thoughts because without real care and love we are all hiding behind a sheer veneer of nothing.

◈ OBSERVATIONS: *mona lisa's house*

I find it most interesting that what consumes most of our thoughts is on autopilot for mental suffering. The judging, the comparing, the competing, and the indulgent consumption; they all seem to take precedence over the basic fact that the miracle of being alive supercedes all those tenfold.

We look
We think
We wonder
We begin to be curious
Yet we look away
We think too fast
We wonder why we look away
We begin to question ourselves
We can touch
We can express
We can reach out
And we can begin to wonder why we're looking
We're thinking
And why we're both so curiously not speaking.

I was intrigued listening in to the small fraction of straight women who think they don't need a man. They certainly know-it-all after having had conquered independence and self-reliance; admirable qualities and good in moderation but there is more to life. But who needs a man, right? They started describing the passion, or certainly lack of, in their life, and treaded around the recognition of a man enhancing their lives. Yet somehow in their illusive badgering they glossed over the reality that the perfume they were wearing, the makeup that flatters and hides their blemishes, the high heels that make them feel sexy and feminine, the bra that keeps the twins at attention, the car that got them here safely and in style, the multitude of innovations that make their life more convenient and comfortable, even the surgeon who made them more attractive and less insecure-- are all compliments of a man and his creative energies and offerings. If you cannot recognize gratitude how will you ever recognize that you really do need a man?

∽ OBSERVATIONS: *mona lisa's house*

Our predominant culture is saturated with communication devices and technological platforms for interaction and contact. We are so accessible, tracked, and conditioned to being located. Yet what is so ironic is that with all we have at our fingertips, we seem to be more out of touch than in touch with each other. Oh right, iknow, itouch is coming...icannotwait.

What happened to the moments when a woman would dress to the nines to get a man's attention and not another woman's envious stare? When the competition for attention between women is strictly between women, the dynamic has nowhere to advance except to a game of imploding chaos.

The love of possessions is a weakness to strengthen. We stuff things in our cars, our closets, our offices, and our homes. Then we stuff more stuff into public storage. The excess appears to be disturbing any sense of spiritual balance of only taking what you need and needing only that which you take. There is nothing wrong with possessions when countered with the awareness of giving; it's okay to let go of some things and taste that happiness. Possessions should not be stored or isolated; they need to be shared. We have to learn to love what we can giveaway.

We assume so much and feel so entitled to even more. It's quite laughable. We think we know but really don't know what we don't know. All I know is I plan to get most everything in my life I didn't plan.

Like many, I have learned to let go of people and say goodbye to what has passed. It is never easy yet I understand the necessity for affirming change and the newfound voice of freedom that follows. Everything is strangely reciprocal when you step away or off the path from someone or something. And although most goodbyes are unusually natural, the most painful goodbyes are the ones that are never said.

The problem with most kids today is their parents. Somehow parents got sidetracked and forgot to teach their kids truth, and most of all, enforce respect. Without both, common sense and socialization has taken a hit. When there is no clear sense of moral boundaries and a lack of generational respect, kids go astray. Our culture's order of authority and humility are blurred lines that parents at one time saw a bit more clear but now pass on muddled in the eyes of their children.

In our suffering there is proof of being alive. And in our aliveness there sits next to us the proof that it will all be taken away. In living you feel matter. In dying you leave matter behind. So what does matter really mean?-- that it's here and now, then gone and left behind? And does it really matter? It's a fascinating cycle to live and die by.

The force of socialization is in looking each other in the eyes; for answers, for questions, for sharing a light of connectivity. We hold now in our hands, different forms of technology that stun our eyes. And deaden our hearts. It's evident in people's inability to smile from deep within and without caution. I have never seen so many well-equipped, beautifully put together and unresponsive people in all my life.

∽ OBSERVATIONS: *mona lisa's house*

Don't settle for anything less than what you really want, and want to give. Strive always for the excellence that manifests from sacrifices. When you settle for less, you give less and that negates the entire exchange for everyone involved; kind of like average sex that never really excites but merely climaxes unannounced.

The measuring of something is relative to its situation and destiny. Why do some have so much and others have so little? And who really decides that? The circumstances of the hand that each of us is dealt is uniquely mind-boggling. What we must recognize is the shoe of happiness and suffering is not the same size for everyone.

One of our biggest misfortunes and miscalculations
is wasting the preciousness of energy through fear.
For fear masks the surface of all that is possible to
experience. So make your fears serve you, not
drain you.

Words are an elixir and a dynamic experience.
Yet it is far beyond the language of words that
captures your attention and desires; it is the unseen
friction and energies that sneak into your imagination
and allow it to run wildly through the fire of
extraordinary exchanges.

~ OBSERVATIONS: *mona lisa's house*

The definition of a secret: something that is kept or meant to be kept unknown or unseen by others. Ironically so, if you ever want to expose more in unexpected coverage and questioning than you ever dreamed possible, keep something a secret.

There is so much pleasure in food as well as consequences. Most of us are food junkies in some way and caught up with behaviors that allow foods to be detrimental and dangerous for our beings. But it's not burgers or French fries, or cokes or processed foods that are distorting us. It's the wedding cake.

We are celebratory creatures seeking enlightenment. In each celebration there is usually some form of an epiphany. Then comes that other sudden illumination when the wine tricks you, and as clear as day, you convince yourself of what you already knew and now celebrate in its folly of awakening.

Diplomacy is the vision to resolve difficult situations with simple approaches. It is really common sense that becomes an applicable art form. After all, an effective artist does not compose a detailed masterpiece with a mop.

∼ Observations: *mona lisa's house*

I know it sounds crazy but I find it hard to fathom that I follow myself around my whole life. I never get a break or vacation or reprieval from me; always thinking and plotting and fantasizing, yet never really escaping any of my thoughts and actions. I realized I could never really ditch myself either although there are a few "mes" that I would like too. And the funny thing is I keep re-inventing those other mes I really don't want to follow.

It is in the doing of something that releases the gripping fear of change and in the non-doing that allows stillness born to action. Many skins must be unleashed, then shed, in the turning over of a new you.

We don't come into the world feet first but head first; kind of odd yet ironic to arrive upside down. We then spend a lifetime finding the balance of our footing and stability in the world upright. In the journey of leaving the womb, where darkness is both home and comforting ally, our most heroic act of courage is summoned to leave that cave. With birth, life forces out each person from that place of ultimate safety to face, then endure the process of evolving. Although we each approach life in so many different ways, the inception for all humans is universally the same: that awareness is born at conception; birth yields to light and shadow; and the unfolding of life's adventures transforms with each step forward. Naturally we come out head first into the world, but knowingly we first test the waters of life with the soles of our feet.

∾ Observations: *mona lisa's house*

So much of life seems waiting to be repeated; perhaps it's there for us to learn to change what is needed to move forward. There are so many road signs in life. Of course one cannot be attentive to all the signals but hopefully to the few that detour one's life on a colorful road of surprises and exhilarating experiences. To repeat adventure would be acceptable; nothing else will be admitted. Life is lived in courage, not in the waiting room.

No one can see his or her reflection in running water so be calm and grateful for what you have as well as what you don't have. One day your life will flash before your eyes. Make sure it's in focus and worth watching.

Sometimes the emptiness of existence tempered with the marvel of life is compassionately eye-opening. For in that moment where we had thought to be alone, we will be with all the world.

CHAPTER 6 Quotes

Quotes
more with less

QUOTES: *more with less*

We all come spinning out of nothingness yet everything in the universe is within us. So hide in my heart like a secret and unveil through whispers the beautiful thoughts and discoveries that leave the unending sky breathless.

I listened to her story. I listened to his story. And then I listened to my story of their stories. I now realize, sometimes you just have to put your head down on the ground and listen to the forest through the leaves.

You have to find the flow or source of your power and use it wisely, as it uses you. It's an equal exchange valued by letting things take their course without need for obstruction.

Everything that will occur in your own life will occur in its own time. You cannot push the river; only feel its current by being its flow.

Acceptance lives in expecting nothing; its benefit comes from what is there and its honor from what is not there.

Beauty always emanates from a light in the heart...it is what makes the happiest women the prettiest and all men handsome gentlemen in knowing just that.

Such polarities to living; seems anything meaningful comes with resistance...until you get out of your own way and realize even meaninglessness is meaningful.

◈ Quotes: *more with less*

It's not ultimately where you go; it's how present you feel when you get there and the gratitude you leave in your wake that calls you back.

We believe to imagine that more is more and less is undesirable. Yet oppositely so is the belief in expecting nothing-- and in turn, receiving the abundance of the unimaginable.

When you learn to live with less, you understand how to appreciate more...and find a great awakening in taking nothing for granted.

Sleep turns to dreams...dreams turn to awakenings... awakenings turn to all that is tangible. The universe knows how to transform anything at all into every thing that's necessary.

Rain does not rain because it has an answer; it rains because it's wet.

I don't yearn for what was nor stress for what will be. I relish in what is present and find the past and the future all taken care of.

Let go of the last year into the silent limbo of the past and ask for not a new year but a new soul.

Don't use your energy to worry.
Use your energy to believe.
And surround yourself with people who believe
in all dreams.

In music, the pause...is as important as the note. It's
quite amazing how listening to nothing can silence the
mind and hear the richness of music.

Tears flow out of both purposefulness and purposelessness. It's remarkable how the body and mind set up
its own climate and control for deep meaning or lack
thereof.

Don't Scratch The Diamond

We live in an impatient world. We want things now and cannot help our self-serving entitlement. I too, am tired of rushing. I don't want to go any faster than the quickest way possible.

I think I mean something to a lot of people but to a few I know I mean a lot.

Peace is not a stretch of the imagination, it is our imagination wanting and willing to be colored in by every human heart. We just keep breeding love through peace.

~ QUOTES: *more with less*

Patience is the cloak from which all nuisances find a different search to provoke.

A revolution takes time to settle in…but only a blink of the eye to ignite.

The more that the truth becomes transparent, the less we believe in what has kept us shadowed in subterfuge. When you straddle the dark it is always transparent to the truth.

Freedom is far more than just doing what you want; it's more about honoring yourself and better sense and not being subjected to the things you don't want.

It is a birthright to be entitled to miracles and to being a magnet for all good things. The force within is the original blueprint for all things unknown to be born known.

We are on track to becoming the most well-informed society to ever die of thoughtlessness without even questioning it.

Anxiety ultimately banishes every trace of joy from life. So don't get too ahead of your thoughts because sometimes a means to an end only sets you nervously back at the beginning.

Human beings tend to focus on the fulfillment of expectations rather than the simple joys of being and then becoming something they never expected to be.

We all need a source of inspiration and a source of aspiration. The time has come to upgrade trust in your own conviction of giving then seeking to give more.

A misconception and miscalculation is that we have forever to live. Never squander your sprinkles of happiness; they are as temporary as your last breath. Every moment is a blessing.

What you are doesn't age. It's what you are not that wrinkles the soul.

Mirror, mirror, on the wall, which reflection is the kindest of them all? The truest light of a mirror is to shine your beauty through the reflection of other people.

Seems many of us are standing on the precipice of the unknown. Adversity truly does introduce us to ourselves.

A chance is something that happens when you step in stride with the finding of what you were looking for but forgot to ask where to find it.

Even in a world where information is the currency of communication, forgetfulness is still a beautiful form of freedom.

Seems we are always being guided in a way better than we know ourselves. The frayed ends of life are tempting to try and mend yet more compelling to leave untouched.

ABOUT THE AUTHOR

David Catrambone was born in Chicago, IL but reared in Los Angeles, CA. He considers himself a true Californian at heart spending a lot of time in the sun culture at Malibu and Zuma beaches, hiking in the Santa Monica Mountains, and skiing and exploring throughout the diverse California experience.

While growing up in Los Angeles, he initially developed skills as a mosaic artist and created many unique multi-media projects for architects, interior designers, and the private sector. From this platform he took his artistic instincts into the entertainment business and worked behind the camera in the production of television and commercials. This is also where he started to develop his passion for writing. He pooled his entertainment experiences and co-founded *Iff*, an international film festival magazine. As publisher and executive editor, he groomed the magazine and traveled the world representing the publication at a multitude of international film festivals and media events.

Today he still lives in Los Angeles, still enjoys the Californian lifestyle, and continues his writing quest in developing a documentary film and television show. He is also very excited to be offering and sharing his first book *Don't Scratch the Diamond*. This collection of original short writings, poems, and quotes is a refreshing and poetic look at humanity and open-hearted journey into life and relationships.